DR. TANYA SMITH

Maximizing Tax Benefits

Phoenix Voices
Uplifting Entrepreneurs

First published by Phoenix Voices Uplifting Entrepreneurs 2025

Second edition

This book was professionally typeset on Reedsy.
Find out more at reedsy.com

Contents

On the other hand, if you treat your business as a business, you have the opportunity to claim a more extensive range of deductions. To establish your endeavor as a business, you need to demonstrate that you're actively engaged in profit-seeking activities. This involves maintaining meticulous records, developing a business plan, and consistently working to promote and monetize your Business.

In conclusion, understanding the tax landscape for Entrepreneurs is a crucial step in building a sustainable Business career. By differentiating between hobby and business and considering the tax implications Entrepreneurs can make informed decisions, optimize their financial strategies, and pave the way for a successful and profitable journey.

Home Office Deductions

The details of defining a home office for tax purposes, calculating the home office deduction, and documenting expenses related to your Business space in this comprehensive guide.

Defining a Home Office for Tax Purposes

In the modern world of remote work and entrepreneurship, the concept of a home office has gained immense importance, not only for convenience but also for its potential tax benefits. For Entrepreneurs like you, who operate from the comfort of your home, understanding what constitutes a home office for tax purposes is the first step in unlocking valuable deductions.

The Exclusive and Regular Use Rule

The IRS has specific criteria for defining a home office eligible for tax deductions. Firstly, the space must be used exclusively and regularly for business activities. This means your home office should be a dedicated area in your residence solely reserved for work related to your business. It should not double as a personal space or serve any other purpose.

Principal Place of Business

Your home office can also be considered your principal place of business if it's where you conduct most of your business activities. In the world of Entrepreneurship, this is often the case, as much of the work, from Business and editing to administrative tasks, is carried out from the home office.

Meeting Clients and Customers

If you meet clients or customers in your home office, it can also meet the criteria for tax purposes. However, keep in mind that the space used for these meetings must be separate from your personal living area.

Calculating the Home Office Deduction

Once you've defined your home office, the next crucial step is calculating the home office deduction, which can lead to significant tax savings for Entrepreneurs like you.

Two Methods

The IRS provides two primary methods for calculating the home office deduction: the Simplified Method and the Regular Method.

Simplified Method

This method is straightforward and involves multiplying the square footage of your home office space (up to 300 square feet) by a prescribed rate set by the IRS. As of my knowledge cutoff in September 2021, the rate was $5 per square foot. This method is easy to use and requires less documentation.

Regular Method

The Regular Method involves calculating the actual expenses associated with your home office, including mortgage or rent, utilities, insurance, and maintenance costs. To use this method, you need to measure the square footage of your home office space and determine the percentage of your home it represents. Then, you can allocate a proportionate share of your expenses as deductions. While more complex, this method can lead to higher deductions for those with larger home offices or substantial expenses.

Documenting Expenses Related to Your Business Space

To claim the home office deduction, meticulous documentation of expenses related to your Business space is paramount. Without proper records, you risk audits and potential issues with the IRS.

Documenting Home Expenses

For the Regular Method, keep records of all relevant home expenses, such as mortgage or rent payments, property taxes, utilities, insurance, and maintenance costs. Be sure to differentiate between expenses for your entire home and those specific to your home office.

Office Expenses

Document expenses directly related to your home office, including office furniture, equipment (such as computers and printers), office supplies, and even repairs or improvements made to your workspace.

Keep a Dedicated Record

Create a separate file or folder specifically for home office expenses. Keep all receipts, invoices, bills, and relevant financial documents organized and easily accessible.

Maintain Consistency

Consistency in your record-keeping is key. Keep track of expenses throughout the year rather than scrambling to gather documents during tax season.

Conclusion

Defining a home office for tax purposes, calculating the home office deduction, and meticulously documenting expenses related to your Business space are essential steps for Entrepreneurs operating a business from home. These processes not only enable you to maximize your tax benefits but also ensure compliance with IRS regulations. Properly managed, your home office can become a financial asset, reducing your tax liability and supporting the growth into a full-time career.

Business and Research Expenses

The intricacies of identifying deductible research expenses, documenting and justifying research costs, and tracking expenses related to Business materials and software in detail. This comprehensive guide will help Entrepreneurs like you make informed decisions about tax deductions.

Identifying Deductible Research Expenses

Research is an integral part of the Entrepreneur's journey, whether you're crafting fiction, non-fiction, or any other form of written work. Understanding which research expenses are deductible can help you maximize your tax benefits.

Books and Publications

One of the most common deductible research expenses is the cost of books, magazines, journals, and other publications directly related to your Business project. This includes reference materials, academic papers, and any materials used to deepen your understanding of your subject matter.

Online Subscriptions

In the digital age, many Entrepreneurs rely on online resources. The costs associated with research databases, e-books, and online subscriptions can often be deducted.

Travel Expenses

If your research necessitates travel, expenses such as airfare, lodging, meals, and transportation can be deductible. This is particularly relevant if you need to visit specific locations, conduct interviews, or gather information firsthand.

Interviews and Expert Fees

When you pay experts or specialists for their insights, interviews, or consultations related to your Business project, these fees are often considered deductible research expenses.

Conference and Seminar Costs

Attending conferences or seminars relevant to your work can also be deductible. This includes registration fees, travel expenses, and accommodation costs.

Software and Digital Tools

Software used for research purposes, such as note-taking applications, research organization tools, and data analysis software, may be eligible for deductions.

Documenting and Justifying Research Costs

While identifying deductible research expenses is essential, proper documentation and justification are equally crucial to ensure your deductions withstand scrutiny.

Maintain Detailed Records

Keep meticulous records of all research-related expenses. This includes receipts, invoices, and any correspondence related to payments or bookings.

Categorize Expenses

Organize your research expenses into clear categories, making it easier to track and justify each deduction. This helps during tax preparation and potential audits.

Prove Relevance

Ensure that every expense you claim as a deduction is directly related to your Business project. Justify the necessity of each expense by demonstrating its relevance to your work.

Keep a Research Journal

Maintain a journal or log where you document your research process, including the materials you accessed, the purpose of your research, and how it contributes to your Business project.

Consult with Experts

When in doubt about whether a particular expense qualifies as a research deduction, consider seeking advice from a tax professional with expertise in Entrepreneurial deductions.

Tracking Expenses Related to Business Materials and Software

Beyond research, Entrepreneurs also incur expenses related to Business materials and software. Properly tracking and documenting these costs can lead to additional deductions.

Office Supplies

Expenses for office supplies like pens, paper, notebooks, and printer ink are deductible. Keep receipts for these items.

Business Software

If you use specialized Business software or word processing tools for your Entrepreneurship, such as Scrivener or Microsoft Word, the costs can be deducted.

Computers and Equipment

The cost of computers, laptops, printers, and other equipment used exclusively or primarily for your Business business is eligible for deductions.

Internet and Phone Expenses

If you use the internet and phone services for your Business and research, a portion of these expenses may be deductible.

Cloud Storage and Backup Services

Expenses for cloud storage or backup services to protect your Business work can often be included as deductions.

Conclusion

Identifying deductible research expenses, documenting and justifying research costs, and tracking expenses related to Business materials and software are essential aspects of managing the financial aspects of your Business career. These practices not only help reduce your tax liability but also ensure you receive the full benefit of available deductions.

Marketing and Promotion

Let's dive into the world of tax-deductible marketing expenses, strategies for maximizing deductions in book promotion, and the considerations around website maintenance and advertising costs for Entrepreneurs into a successful full-time career.

Tax-Deductible Marketing Expenses

Effective marketing is crucial for Entrepreneurs and publishers to reach their audience and promote their work. Understanding which marketing expenses can be tax-deductible can provide significant financial benefits.

Advertising Costs

Advertising expenses are often tax-deductible. This includes expenditures on online ads, social media promotions, pay-per-click advertising, and traditional advertising methods like print ads or billboards.

Book Launch Events

Expenses related to book launch events, including venue rental, catering, and promotional materials, may be eligible for deductions if they are primarily for promoting your books.

Promotional Materials

Costs associated with promotional items like bookmarks, fliers, posters, and branded merchandise can often be deducted.

Publicity and Public Relations

Fees paid to publicists or public relations firms to help promote your work are generally considered deductible marketing expenses.

Website Expenses

The expenses related to creating and maintaining an website, including design, hosting, and content management, can be deductible.

Social Media Management

If you hire professionals or use software to manage your social media presence for promotional purposes, these costs may qualify as deductions.

Strategies for Maximizing Deductions in Book Promotion

While many marketing expenses are eligible for deductions, Entrepreneurs and publishers can employ strategies to maximize these deductions effectively.

Keep Detailed Records

Maintain meticulous records of all marketing expenses, including receipts, invoices, and contracts. This documentation is crucial during tax season.

Categorize Expenses

Organize your marketing expenses into categories such as online advertising, event promotions, and public relations. This categorization streamlines the deduction process.

Separate Personal and Business Expenses

Ensure clear separation between personal and business expenses. Only claim deductions for expenses directly related to promoting your business.

Stay Informed

Keep up-to-date with changes in tax laws and regulations that may impact your eligibility for deductions. Consulting with a tax professional who specializes in Entrepreneurship is wise.

Website Maintenance and Advertising Costs

Website maintenance and advertising are integral components of book promotion in the digital age. Let's explore how these expenses can be tax-deductible.

Websites

Your business website serves as a central hub for your online presence. Expenses related to its creation, hosting, domain registration, and ongoing maintenance can often be deducted. Justify these costs by emphasizing the website's role in promoting your books and engaging with your readers.

Content Creation

If you hire content creators, designers, or Business owners to generate website content or promotional materials, their fees may be tax-deductible, as long as the content is primarily intended for promotion.

Advertising Costs

As mentioned earlier, expenses related to advertising, including online ads, social media promotions, and even promotional campaigns on platforms are typically tax-deductible. Link these costs directly to your marketing efforts.

Email Marketing

Investments in email marketing tools and services used for newsletters and promotional campaigns can often be deducted as marketing expenses.

Search Engine Optimization (SEO)

Expenses for SEO services to enhance the discoverability of your website can qualify as deductions, as they aim to increase your business visibility.

Conclusion

Understanding tax-deductible marketing expenses, strategies for maximizing deductions in promotion, and the considerations surrounding website maintenance and advertising costs is essential for Entrepreneurs looking to optimize their financial strategies. By leveraging these deductions effectively, Entrepreneurs can invest more in promoting their business and growing into a full-time career while managing their tax liability in a smart and compliant manner.

Professional Services

Deducting fees paid to editors, cover designers, and other professionals, understanding the contracts and documentation requirements associated with these services, and the considerations involved in handling payments to freelancers and contractors.

Deducting Fees Paid to Editors, Cover Designers, and Other Professionals

Collaboration with professionals is often crucial for Entrepreneurs and publishers to produce high-quality books. Deducting the fees paid to these experts can significantly impact your finances. Let's explore which professionals' fees are deductible:

Editors

Entrepreneurs often hire editors to review and edit their manuscripts for grammar, style, and content. These editing fees are typically deductible as they directly contribute to the production of your books.

Graphic Designers

Engaging graphic designers to create eye-catching graphics is common in any business. Fees paid to graphic designers can be claimed as deductions since graphics play a vital role in marketing and sales.

Marketing and Publicity Experts

Hiring marketing or publicity professionals to promote your books can lead to increased sales. Fees paid to these experts are often considered deductible marketing expenses.

Ghostwriters

Entrepreneurs who collaborate with ghostwriters to create content may also deduct their fees. It's important to ensure that the ghostwriters contract specifies the work's nature and ownership.

Web Designers and Developers

For Entrepreneurs with websites dedicated to their work, fees paid to web designers and developers for website creation and maintenance are often deductible.

Understanding Contracts and Documentation Requirements

Properly understanding contracts and meeting documentation requirements is crucial when engaging with professionals in the industry. Here's what you need to consider:

Clear Contracts

Each professional engagement should be governed by a clear contract specifying the scope of work, deadlines, payment terms, and ownership rights. Contracts are essential for protecting your interests and documenting the professional relationship.

Retain Invoices and Receipts

Maintain copies of all invoices and receipts related to professional fees. These documents serve as evidence of expenses and are vital for tax purposes.

Record Communications

Keep records of email exchanges, communication logs, and any correspondence related to the services provided. These records can help clarify any disputes or questions about the work.

Ownership Rights

In contracts with professionals like ghostwriter owners or illustrators, clarify ownership rights to avoid legal complications. Ensure the contract clearly states who owns the content or artwork produced.

Compliance with Tax Laws

Be aware of any tax obligations related to payments to professionals. Depending on their employment status, you may need to withhold taxes or issue appropriate tax forms like 1099s.

Handling Payments to Freelancers and Contractors

Efficiently handling payments to freelancers and contractors is crucial to maintain professionalism and ensure accurate financial records. Here are essential steps to consider:

Payment Agreements

Agree upon payment terms in advance. Determine the amount, due date, and method of payment. Clearly communicate these terms to the professional.

Invoicing

Request invoices from the professionals you engage with. Invoices should detail the services provided, fees, and payment instructions.

Payment Records

Maintain a systematic record of all payments made to freelancers and contractors. This record should include the date, recipient, amount, and purpose of each payment.

Retain Tax Forms

If required by tax regulations, ensure you collect necessary tax forms from professionals, such as W-9 forms, to report payments accurately.

Track Expenses

Categorize professional fees as business expenses and ensure they are accurately recorded in your financial records.

Prepare for Tax Reporting

As the end of the tax year approaches, prepare for tax reporting by ensuring all payment records and necessary documentation are in order.

Conclusion

Deducting fees paid to editors, graphic designers, and other professionals requires a clear understanding of contracts, documentation requirements, and payment handling processes. By following these guidelines, Entrepreneurs can navigate these financial transactions effectively while growing their business into a full-time career. Proper documentation, compliance with tax laws, and clear communication with professionals are key to ensuring a successful and financially responsible journey.

Travel and Conferences

Eligible travel expenses for Entrepreneurs, documenting and justifying travel-related deductions, and navigating the complexities of conference expenses.

Eligible Travel Expenses for Entrepreneurs

Travel is often an integral part of an Entrepreneur's journey, whether it's for research, book signings, or attending literary events. Understanding which travel expenses can be considered eligible for deductions can provide valuable financial benefits. Here's a breakdown of common eligible travel expenses:

Transportation Costs

- Airfare or train tickets: Expenses for flights or train journeys directly related to your Entrepreneurship work.
- Mileage: If you use your personal vehicle for business travel, you can often deduct mileage expenses at the IRS-approved rate.
- Rental cars: Costs associated with renting a car for business purposes.

Lodging Expenses

- Hotel or lodging fees: Accommodation costs during your business travel can be deductible.
- Airbnb or vacation rentals: Expenses for rental properties can also qualify if they are used for business purposes.

Meals and Entertainment

- Meals: Generally, 50% of the cost of meals during business travel is deductible.
- Entertainment: Expenses for entertaining clients, publishers, or business associates during your travels can be eligible.

Conference and Event Registration Fees

- Registration fees for conferences, book fairs, and literary events that you attend as part of your Entrepreneurship business.

Research-Related Travel

- Expenses for travel associated with gathering research materials or conducting interviews for your Business projects.

Documenting and Justifying Travel-Related Deductions

Proper documentation and justification of travel-related deductions are vital to ensure compliance with tax regulations and maximize your tax benefits. Here's how to do it effectively:

Maintain a Detailed Travel Diary

- Keep a travel diary or log where you record the purpose of your trip, dates, destinations, and business-related activities.

Keep Receipts and Invoices

- Retain all receipts, invoices, and bills related to your travel expenses. These documents serve as evidence of your expenditures.

Categorize Expenses

- Organize your travel expenses into categories such as transportation, lodging, meals, and conference fees for clarity during tax preparation.

Justify Business Purpose

- Ensure that each travel expense is directly related to your Entrepreneurship business. Clearly demonstrate how each expense contributes to your work.

Collect Supporting Documents

- Gather supporting documents such as conference agendas, event schedules, and meeting notes to substantiate the business nature of your travel.

Navigating the Complexities of Conference Expenses

Conferences are significant events for Entrepreneurs and publishers, offering networking opportunities, learning experiences, and promotional potential. However, understanding the intricacies of conference expenses and deductions is essential:

Registration Fees

- Registration fees for conferences and literary events are typically deductible. Ensure you keep records of your registration confirmations and payment receipts.

Travel and Lodging

- Expenses related to travel and lodging, such as airfare, hotel stays, and transportation to and from the conference venue, are often deductible.

Meals and Entertainment

- As mentioned earlier, you can generally deduct 50% of the cost of meals and entertainment during business travel, including conference-related expenses.

Materials and Promotional Items

- Expenses for promotional materials, business cards, and books you distribute at conferences can be considered deductible marketing expenses.

Networking and Education

- Justify conference expenses by emphasizing the educational and networking opportunities they offer. Be prepared to explain how attending the conference benefits your Entrepreneurship business.

6. Travel Extensions

- If you extend your stay for personal reasons, be cautious about which expenses can still be considered deductible. Only expenses directly related to the business portion of your trip qualify.

Conclusion

Navigating eligible travel expenses for Entrepreneurs, documenting and justifying travel-related deductions, and handling the complexities of conference expenses require attention to detail and a clear understanding of tax regulations. Proper documentation and transparency are key to successful and responsible financial management in the world of Entrepreneurship.

Equipment and Depreciation

Depreciating office equipment like computers and printers, tracking and documenting equipment purchases, and the tax implications of leasing versus buying equipment.

Depreciating Office Equipment

Office equipment such as computers, printers, and other devices are essential tools for Entrepreneurs and publishers. Understanding how to depreciate these assets can help you optimize your financial strategy. Here's what you need to know:

Depreciation Basics

- Depreciation is a tax deduction that allows you to spread the cost of a tangible asset (like office equipment) over its useful life, rather than deducting the full cost in the year of purchase.
- Computers, printers, and similar equipment typically have a predetermined "useful life" set by the IRS, which can vary depending on the type of asset.

MACRS Depreciation

- Most office equipment falls under the Modified Accelerated Cost Recovery System (MACRS) for depreciation. MACRS assigns a specific depreciation method and recovery period to different types of assets.
- For instance, computers are generally assigned a 5-year recovery period, while printers might have a 7-year recovery period.

Depreciation Deduction

- You can deduct a portion of the equipment's cost each year over its useful life. This reduces your taxable income, lowering your overall tax liability.

Tracking and Documenting Equipment Purchases

Properly tracking and documenting your equipment purchases is crucial for accurate depreciation deductions and maintaining organized financial records. Here's how to do it effectively:

Maintain Purchase Records

- Keep detailed records of all equipment purchases, including invoices, receipts, and payment records. These documents should clearly state the date, description of the equipment, cost, and the seller's information.

Create an Asset Register

- Maintain an asset register or list that includes all equipment purchased for your business. Include relevant details such as purchase date, purchase price, and the asset's description.

Categorize Equipment

- Categorize your equipment purchases accurately. Different types of equipment may have different depreciation schedules and recovery periods, impacting your deductions.

Keep Track of Improvements

- If you make improvements or upgrades to existing equipment, document these changes and adjust the asset's value accordingly.

Consult a Tax Professional

- Seek guidance from a tax professional or accountant with expertise in depreciation and asset management to ensure compliance with tax regulations and optimize your deductions.

Tax Implications of Leasing vs. Buying Equipment

Deciding whether to lease or buy office equipment can have significant tax implications. Each option comes with its own set of considerations:

Leasing Equipment

- Lease payments are typically considered operational expenses and are fully deductible in the year they're paid.
- Leasing can provide flexibility in upgrading to newer equipment, but you won't own the asset, and over time, leasing may cost more than buying.

Buying Equipment

- When you purchase equipment, you can depreciate its cost over its useful life, spreading the deduction over several years.
- Owning equipment gives you long-term value, and you can often claim depreciation deductions even beyond the equipment's cost.

Considerations

- The decision between leasing and buying depends on your financial situation and business needs. Leasing may provide immediate tax benefits, while buying may offer long-term value.

Conclusion

Depreciating office equipment, tracking and documenting equipment purchases, and understanding the tax implications of leasing versus buying equipment are critical aspects of managing the financial side of your business. By following these guidelines and seeking professional advice when necessary. Properly managed assets and financial records are key to long-term financial success in the world of Entrepreneurship.

Health Insurance and Retirement

Health insurance deductions for self-employed Entrepreneurs, retirement account options and their tax benefits, and the art of balancing current financial needs with long-term planning.

Health Insurance Deductions for Self-Employed Entrepreneurs

Health insurance is a critical aspect of financial planning for self-employed Entrepreneurs. Understanding how to deduct health insurance expenses can provide significant tax benefits. Here's what you need to know:

Self-Employed Health Insurance Deduction

- Self-employed individuals, including Entrepreneurs and publishers, can often deduct the cost of health insurance premiums for themselves, their spouses, and their dependents.
- This deduction is typically available even if you don't itemize your deductions.

Qualifications

- To qualify for the self-employed health insurance deduction, you must meet specific criteria. You must be self-employed with a net profit, and your health plan must be established under your business, or you must be considered a partner or shareholder in an S corporation.

Deduction Limits

- The deduction is generally limited to your net profit from self-employment. You can't claim a deduction that would result in a net loss from your Business activities.

Reporting on Tax Forms

- You'll report your self-employed health insurance deduction on your tax return, typically on Form 1040.

Retirement Account Options and Tax Benefits

Planning for retirement is essential, even for self-employed Entrepreneurs. Various retirement account options offer tax benefits that can help you secure your financial future. Here are some common options:

Individual Retirement Accounts (IRAs)

- Traditional IRA: Contributions are often tax-deductible, and earnings grow tax-deferred until withdrawal, usually in retirement.

- Roth IRA: Contributions are not tax-deductible, but qualified withdrawals are tax-free, offering tax-free growth potential.

Simplified Employee Pension (SEP) IRA

- SEP IRAs are designed for self-employed individuals and small business owners.
- Contributions are tax-deductible, and the plan allows for higher contribution limits compared to traditional IRAs.

Solo 401(k)

- Also known as a one-participant or individual 401(k), this plan is designed for self-employed individuals with no employees other than a spouse.
- Contributions are tax-deductible, and the plan offers higher contribution limits than IRAs.

Simplified Employee Pension (SIMPLE) IRA

- Suitable for small businesses, including self-employed individuals.
- Contributions are tax-deductible, and there are lower administrative requirements compared to other retirement plans.

Tax Benefits

- Contributions to these retirement accounts are often tax-deductible, reducing your taxable income for the year.

- Investment earnings within these accounts grow tax-deferred, allowing your savings to potentially compound more quickly.

Balancing Current Needs with Long-Term Financial Planning

Balancing your current financial needs with long-term planning can be challenging but is crucial for financial stability and success. Here are strategies to achieve this balance:

Create a Budget

- Establish a budget that allocates a portion of your income to current expenses and another portion to savings and investments, including retirement accounts.

Emergency Fund

- Build an emergency fund to cover unexpected expenses, ensuring you don't need to dip into long-term savings for emergencies.

Set Financial Goals

- Define clear financial goals, both short-term and long-term. Prioritize these goals and align your financial decisions accordingly.

Regularly Review Finances

- Periodically review your financial situation and adjust your budget and savings plan as needed to accommodate changes in income, expenses, and goals.

Professional Guidance

- Consider working with a financial advisor or accountant who specializes in self-employed individuals and Entrepreneurs to ensure your financial plan is tailored to your unique situation.

Conclusion

Understanding health insurance deductions, exploring retirement account options, and mastering the art of balancing current financial needs with long-term planning are essential aspects of managing your financial journey as a self-employed Entrepreneur and publisher. By following these guidelines and making informed financial decisions, Entrepreneurs can secure their financial future while successfully pursuing their business careers growing them into a full-time endeavor. Effective financial planning and discipline are key to achieving both short-term goals and long-term financial security.

Record-Keeping and Compliance

Let's explore best practices for record-keeping and staying organized and prepared for tax season. Effective record-keeping is essential for Entrepreneurs aiming to manage their finances efficiently.

Best Practices for Record-Keeping

Maintaining organized and thorough records is the foundation of successful financial management. Here are best practices to follow:

Create a Dedicated Workspace

- Establish a dedicated space for financial records, whether it's a physical filing cabinet or a digital folder structure on your computer. This will help keep your documents organized and easily accessible.

Use Accounting Software

- Consider using accounting software designed for small

businesses or self-employed individuals. These tools can automate many record-keeping tasks and streamline financial management.

Separate Business and Personal Finances

- Keep your personal and business finances separate. Maintain separate bank accounts and credit cards for your business to avoid commingling funds.

Categorize Expenses

- Categorize expenses accurately. Use categories that align with your specific business needs, such as research, marketing, office supplies, and professional fees.

Maintain Detailed Receipts

- Keep all receipts, invoices, and bills related to your business expenses. Digital copies are acceptable, but make sure they are easily searchable and organized.

Document Income

- Record all sources of income, including book sales, royalties, speaking engagements, and freelance work. Clearly note the date and amount received.

Record Transactions Promptly

- Make it a habit to record financial transactions as soon as they occur. This ensures accuracy and reduces the risk of forgetting or misplacing important information.

Regular Reconciliation

- Reconcile your bank and credit card statements regularly to ensure that your records match your financial institution's records.

Back Up Digital Records

- If you rely on digital record-keeping, regularly back up your data to prevent loss in case of computer failure or data corruption.

Seek Professional Guidance

Consult with a tax professional or accountant who specializes in self-employed individuals to ensure that you are maintaining records in compliance with tax regulations.

Staying Organized and Prepared for Tax Season

As tax season approaches, being organized and prepared can help you avoid last-minute stress and ensure accurate tax filings. Here's how to stay on top of your finances:

Maintain a Tax Calendar

- Create a tax calendar that includes important deadlines

for quarterly estimated tax payments, filing dates, and any tax-related documentation submissions.

Organize Tax Documents

- Gather all necessary tax documents, such as 1099s, W-2s, and any other income-related forms. Keep them in a designated folder or envelope.

Review Deductions

- Review your business expenses and deductions to ensure you've claimed all eligible deductions. This includes expenses related to research, marketing, office space, and health insurance.

Estimate Tax Payments

- If you make quarterly estimated tax payments, calculate and submit these payments on time to avoid penalties and interest.

Consult a Tax Professional

- Consider seeking professional assistance for tax preparation. An experienced tax advisor can help you maximize deductions and ensure accurate filings.

Double-Check Before Filing

- Review your tax return carefully before filing. Verify that all information is accurate, including income, deductions, and personal details.

Keep Records for Several Years

- Retain copies of your tax returns and supporting documentation for at least three to seven years, as this is typically the time frame during which the IRS may audit your returns.

Electronic Filing

- Consider electronically filing your tax return. E-filing is secure, efficient, and often results in quicker refunds.

Plan Ahead for Next Year

- Use the lessons learned from this tax season to plan ahead for the next one. Implement improvements to your record-keeping and financial management processes.

Conclusion

Effective record-keeping and staying organized for tax season are fundamental to the financial success of Entrepreneurs , striving to turn their passion into a full-time career. By following these best practices and maintaining discipline in financial management, you can navigate the complexities of self-employment, minimize tax liability, and achieve long-term financial stability in the world of Entrepreneurship. Properly managed records and proactive tax preparation are key to your financial well-being and business growth.

Tax Strategies and Planning

Year-round tax planning for Entrepreneurs, strategies for minimizing tax liability, and the importance of consulting with tax professionals and experts. Effective tax planning is crucial.

Year-Round Tax Planning for Entrepreneurs

Successful tax planning is a year-round effort that goes beyond the tax season. Here's how to approach it:

Set Up an Effective Record-Keeping System

- Year-round tax planning starts with organized records. Maintain a well-structured system for tracking income and expenses throughout the year.

Quarterly Estimated Tax Payments

- As a self-employed Entrepreneur, you may need to make quarterly estimated tax payments to cover your federal and state income tax liabilities. Calculate these payments accurately and submit them on time.

Monitor Income Streams

- Keep a close eye on your various income streams, including book sales, royalties, speaking engagements, and freelance work. This helps you anticipate and manage your tax obligations.

Track Deductions

- Continuously track and categorize business expenses that qualify for deductions, such as marketing costs, research expenses, and office supplies. Maintaining accurate records is vital.

Regularly Review Tax Laws

- Tax laws and regulations change. Stay informed about any updates or changes that may impact your tax situation. Consulting with a tax professional can help you stay compliant.

Maximize Retirement Contributions

- Consider contributing to retirement accounts like IRAs or solo 401(k)s. These contributions can reduce your taxable income and help you save for the future.

Strategies for Minimizing Tax Liability

Minimizing tax liability is a key goal for any self-employed Entrepreneur. Here are effective strategies:

Deduct Eligible Business Expenses

- Ensure you claim all eligible business expenses as deductions. This includes expenses related to research, marketing, home office costs, and health insurance premiums.

Leverage Tax Credits

- Explore tax credits available for Entrepreneurs and publishers. For instance, you may qualify for the Earned Income Tax Credit (EITC) or the Child Tax Credit, depending on your circumstances.

Optimize Retirement Contributions

- Contribute the maximum allowed to retirement accounts like IRAs or solo 401(k)s. These contributions reduce your taxable income and help secure your financial future.

Manage Self-Employment Tax

- Self-employed individuals are subject to self-employment tax, which covers Social Security and Medicare. Explore strategies to minimize this tax burden, such as deducting one-half of the self-employment tax.

Consider Legal Entity

- Depending on your business structure, you may have options to reduce taxes. Consult with a tax professional to determine if changing your business entity could be beneficial.

Tax-Loss Harvesting

- If you have investments, consider tax-loss harvesting to offset gains with losses, reducing your overall tax liability.

Timing of Income and Expenses

- Manage the timing of your income and expenses to your advantage. For instance, defer income or accelerate expenses when it makes sense for your tax situation.

Consulting with Tax Professionals and Experts

Seeking professional guidance is essential for effective tax planning. Here's why it's crucial:

Expertise and Knowledge

- Tax professionals and experts have in-depth knowledge of tax laws and regulations. They can help you navigate complex tax situations.

Personalized Advice

- A tax professional can assess your unique financial situation and provide tailored advice and strategies to minimize tax liability.

Compliance Assurance

- Tax professionals ensure that you remain in compliance with tax laws, reducing the risk of audits or penalties.

Maximizing Deductions

- Tax experts can identify deductions and credits you might overlook, helping you maximize your tax savings.

Long-Term Planning

- Tax professionals can assist with long-term financial planning, including retirement and estate planning.

Conclusion

Year-round tax planning, strategies for minimizing tax liability, and consulting with tax professionals are essential components of financial management for self-employed Entrepreneurs. Effective tax planning is a cornerstone of financial success in the world of Entrepreneurship.